Memory Care

poems by

Matthew Chronister

Finishing Line Press
Georgetown, Kentucky

Memory Care

For my family

ACKNOWLEDGMENTS

The author would like to thank the editors of the following publications in
which some of these poems have appeared:

Suisun Valley Review: "In November"
Sacramento Voices: "Numb"
Poetry Now: "Balance"
8-West Press: "Yield"
Calaveras Station Literary Journal: "Betty's Flowers"

Publisher: Leah Maines
Editor: Christen Kincaid
Cover Art: Brienna Edwards
Author Photo: Brienna Edwards

Printed in the USA on acid-free paper.
Order online: www.finishinglinepress.com
also available on amazon.com

Author inquiries and mail orders:
Finishing Line Press
P. O. Box 1626
Georgetown, Kentucky 40324
U. S. A.

Table of Contents

The Rounds

Helping Gerry down the hall
of the Memory Care Unit to
the dining room,
she says to me,

> "Where am I?
> > This isn't home.
> Where am I?
> > This isn't home.

> Where am I?"

Later, I come around
to check her plate.
She's pushed around potatoes,
cut up chicken
but hasn't eaten either.
"Why aren't you eating?"
I ask, and she replies,

> "This isn't home.
> > Where am I?"

Still, later,
headed back to her room,
she asks again,

> "Where am I?
> > This isn't home.
> Where am I?"

I show her around her room,
the pictures on the walls—
she can list them all:
"That's me as a girl. Mom and Daddy.
Mitch before we married."

But the next day, when
her daughter arrives,
Gerry asks,

"Where

        am

            I?"

In November

when golden leaves had gathered
on the lawn, grandmother's gardener, Jesùs,
would rake them into large piles,
while singing.

She slept through mornings then,
well into afternoons. But the first time he sang
outside her sills,
clearing the leaves from her flower bed,
she woke up early.

We expected her to be angry.
Instead, she took her cup of coffee,
sat on the porch
and listened.

Before long,
from her spot on the couch
or as she moved about the house
we'd hear her hum the melodies
of the hymns that woke her.

Yield

Among the few able to leave of their
own accord, Mable, who drove a Cadillac
Deville, mistook the gas pedal for the brake
and looked aghast, when suddenly
her front end rested against an entryway
pillar, left with a dent. Mable's body was bruised
from the restraint; as was her
pride. We watched her deflate like the airbag
when moved from the wreck to a gurney;
she'd become upset that the day
she was frightened to see, was already here—
she gave up license and keys to her family,
chose to surrender her freedom for fear
her fender might meet something softer than stone

Too Late

After a brief hospital stay, Grandpa is in
a Skilled Nursing Facility, where for a length of time,
he's been sent to regain strength— still shows strength of mind.

The pant-suit behind the desk
requests he not be gone too long:

"Visiting hours normally end at eight,
but if he isn't out too late, we'll make an exception."

Grandpa replies:
"I should hope so since my wife is dying."

In the hospital's Neuro ICU, after a massive stroke
Grandma has tubes up her nose and down
her throat. Her chest inflates mechanically, while
hear heart rate spikes and falls.
Grandpa sits at her bedside all night.

The following morning, staring at the pile
of files, the scattered papers of their plans for this
moment, even the strangest things seem
routine: Call the doctor into the room,
                                 shake the sterile hand,
                                 scrawl the signature in ballpoint,
                                 tell him to remove the tubes,
                                 stay in place—
                                 until the last gravely rattle escapes.

The King

"This is a cathouse you know?"
Henry says, looking over the frame of his glasses.
"My first night, two women fought over me.
The younger one won."

A bell rings from another room.
"Hear that?" he whispers, "that bell?"
"It's how they call the girls."

Two women in burgundy scrubs and latex
gloves rush down the hall.
"There they go! See how they run over?"

Henry grabs the rail on the wheel of his wheelchair,
inching himself closer.
"They'll do this all night! I watch them come and go!"

Hearing the footfall of his nurse approaching,
Henry is quickly quiet.
 "Do you need anything else?"
she asks from the doorway.

Dismissing her question, he sends her away,
his back straight, robe
draped around his shoulders,
and arms resting on both sides of his seat,
but not before saying,
"I'll call when I do."

Balance

Preparing to be discharged
from the Skilled Nursing Facility,
Grandpa refuses help.

I hold his arm to steady him
like a father holding the hand of a toddler.
He swats my hands away.

His shaking arms push his walker
while his slippers scrape
the concrete, each step long and

drawn out. With every step, he sucks
a large breath and pauses, resting
himself on the walker,
hunching over the steel bars.

Finally calling for the wheelchair,
he sets himself upon the seat and lets his feet drag
as I push him to the car.

Unable to grasp the buckle,
I stretch the belt across his body
and strap him in.

We ride home in silence. On the sidewalk,
a young father pushes a bicycle
while his son pedals.

Backfire

Claire, who once
could care
for herself,
 is now under
constant supervision.

She had been
removed from her
home by her
family and
was placed in
Independent Living.
Nurses monitored
her medicines,
but she was
free to do as she
pleased, including
cooking in
the kitchenette.

The day that
Claire was sent
to Memory Care,
rumors spread like
flames from
the newspaper
she'd set
on her stove.

A group that
gathered weekly
to play poker
laid opinions
like winning hands.

"She meant to
set that fire."
"She did it
to get back
at her daughter
for putting
her here."
"She thought her
family would
move her in
with them."

The Slow Decline

When we returned some weeks after she died,
the house began to show its age:
the shingle siding cracking, coming loose,
covered with dirt, the paint peeling—
the faded tan of terracotta pots
that baked for decades during sunny summers
in grandma's garden. Twenty years ago,
her husband laid the stone walkway by hand,
had us grandchildren write our names and ages
before the concrete dried. The same carvings
now masked by weeds as if we didn't grow
up here. Inside, the little living room
held Christmas after Christmas. During winter months
we'd huddle around the wall heater, our hands
outstretched while it clanged and piped out waves of heat.
And down the narrow hall, the walls still hold
the pictures of our youth: my baby cousin
sitting on Grandma's knee, she beaming at him.
The spare bedroom is full of porcelain
figures to be packed, their blank expressions
covered with dust. For years Grandpa would take
the family out to find these dolls for Grandma.
Unable to help these days, he sits and waits
for me to reduce his life to stacks of boxes.

Betty's Flowers

Betty sits at a table by the window,
alone. I shuffle through a maze of walkers and wheelchairs
that crowd the dining room,
making my way towards her.
As I take her order, her trembling arm reaches for her glass.
"More water please," she asks, extending her cup
to the edge of the table.

 Her arms show signs of a fall, red and yellow bruises.
"What happened Betty?" I ask, refilling her water.
"I've lost my balance lately," she says.

She empties her glass
without ever taking a drink.
Holding her glass to the lip of the vase on her table,
she pours the water slowly,
wetting stems that are always green,
admiring petals made of cloth.

Noticing my stare, she asks with a smile,
"Aren't they beautiful? I've been watering them daily."

Cost of Living

Knowing she couldn't provide
the level of care Grandpa needed,
Mom began searching for care homes.

1. Mountain Manor
Outside, the first stop is guarded—
a man asks our reason for visiting
before allowing us through the wrought-iron gates.

As we enter, we're surprised:
The roadway leads us around
several fountains and green, sprawling lawns.

A nurse pushes a patient in a wheelchair outside,
while a groundskeeper groups
fallen leaves with his leaf blower.

The entrance has large doors
of oak and glass, and we're greeted
by the manager. She leads the tour

through the building, shows us
the decorated dining room,
an extensive exercise facility

and more. The only room she has
available is large. With the curtains
pulled back it's flooded with sunlight.

She is quick to point out that
outside, we can see the bobbing heads
of rose blossoms in the breeze.

In the manager's office we discuss
the price: Medicare will only cover
a fraction of the cost.

In the car, Mom scratches
a thin black line through the top of the list
and we leave for the next location.

2. Atria Gardens
The second stop is smaller.
There is no guard, no gate—
and only a small roundabout at the entrance.

A car is parked there.
A pearlescent Chrysler 300-C
with the company's logo on the door.

The doors are still oak
but on the other side is a receptionist
who will be our guide.

We're shown smaller but similar
rooms; a dining area less grand.
PT is only once a week.

The room where he'd be staying
is smaller—from the bed
there's a view of a patio outside.

When we meet the manager,
she has good news:
Medicare could cover half the cost.

Walking back to the car,
a property sign catches my eye:
It advertises the rooms and care available,

but on the top, white letters
against a red background read:
GRANDMA'S & GRANDPA'S WANTED.

3. ~~College Oaks Care Home~~
At our final stop, the small lot is full
and some cars are double parked.
We are forced to park curbside.

The sliding glass doors open as we approach,
but no one is at the desk.
We ring a bell. No response.

As we show ourselves down the hall
we're greeted with the distinct scent
of urine. It grows stronger as we go further.

At the nurse's station, the head nurse
reviews our files. She's been on for fourteen hours
covering for the manager.

Some residents sit outside
their rooms, and as the nurse leads us,
their gray faces trace our steps.

She leads us down the hall,
down—past groaning patients in cramped confines,
down—into the depths of the building.

There are two rooms available,
both the same: two beds to a room,
divided by a thin curtain.

The one we're shown has a faint
rust-colored stain where the wall
and the ceiling join.

Escorting us to the entrance,
she is sure Medicare will cover the cost
and that Grandpa would love it here.

Cowardice

My first time on the second
        floor of the Memory Care Unit,
                I was sent to bring a lunch

to Ray, a World War II vet,
        who always started conversation
                with "Hey, Tiger." I was laughing

with a nurse about the wallpaper,
        a pale yellow with potted plants,
                when I leaned against the stainless steel

push-bar door handle. I didn't know
        it was armed, meant to go off if pushed
                without entering a code. I stared

at the nurse, at her disbelief, her rush to silence
        the alarm, calm the panicked patients.
                A woman sobbed from another room, and down

the hall—a scream from deep in the diaphragm,
        while Ray, white with terror triggered by the
                piercing wail, stood, trembling, watching,

as I turned my back in panic
        and fled my assignment, leaving him
                there, while I escaped down the stairwell.

Flip-flop

Grandpa's toe is infected, inflamed, oozing pus.
Doctors have treated it,
nurses tend to it,
but it has yet to heal.

Moccasin slippers cover his feet. Fur lined,
soft, easy to walk in. But
the upper rubs against the sore toe.
Ow! Ow! That hurts, he protests.
His daughter grasps one slipper, eases it from his heel
then slides it from the rest of the foot
exposing the pale green lump of the toe.

He needs shoes
that won't rub against the infection.

Here, Dad, try this, my uncle says, offering him his flip-flop.
The V-like straps avoid the joints.
How does that feel, Dad? my mother asks.
It hurts!
Where?
Here? touching the arch of his foot,
Here? now on his big toe.

She repeats the question while we urge him to respond.

I've ALREADY told you three times,
he blurts out,
The bottom of my foot hurts.

Dad, that makes no sense, his son says,
*You haven't even put your foot down
on the floor to know that.*
After some encouraging, he stands to try out the new shoe.
Using his walker he takes a few steps, then retreats
to the comfort of his wheelchair.

I like this. Where's the other one? he asks.
Left foot still in a moccasin, right foot in the flip-flop,
Grandpa stands again,
and slides his foot into the other sandal placed before him.
These are great!

Okay Dad, we'll get you some of these.
Can I have my shoes back now?
Grandpa shouts,
Can someone give him back his shoes?

Numb

Morning shift.
The 8 A.M. crowd
shuffles in
and I rush from
table to table filling
cups with fresh coffee
from an insulated carafe.

Frances grasps her cup
with ring-studded,
wrinkled hands
and with a smile, says,
"This will warm them."
But when the coffee's poured
she looks, annoyed,
and says, "This isn't hot enough."

I assure her, I'll pour another
cup, straight from our brewer
and that will be plenty hot.

I return, my palms red
from grasping the steaming cup,
and place it before her.
Taking it in her hands
again, she sighs
and says,
"Still not hot enough."

No problem.
I've got a plan.
I take it back
and run the cup through
the industrial dishwasher
that heats at
four hundred fifty degrees,

and when it's dry,
I fill the scalded porcelain
with boiling coffee
and bring it to her.
Her rings clink against
the mug, and she
cradles it for a while.
Success.

Until she says,
"Put it in the microwave."

After the microwave's
final beep,
I return from the kitchen,
holding the cup
with a hot mitt
underneath.
For a moment,
I fear the coffee
might be too hot for her
to drink, and wonder if I
should let it cool.

But after I set it on the table
Frances extends
her boney forefinger,
dips it into
the scalding cup of coffee
and asks,

"Is that the best you can do?"

Matthew Chronister is from Sacramento, CA where he works with local youth and writes poetry. He is completing a Master's degree in English at California State University, Sacramento, where he also teaches First Year Composition. His work has appeared in *Poetry Now, Suisun Valley Review* and *8-West Press.*

CPSIA information can be obtained
at www.ICGtesting.com
Printed in the USA
LVHW031724300120
645336LV00016B/1426

9 781646 620999